AGAINST ALL
Odds

---◆---

SHULTZ'S STORY

A COMPELLING STORY OF THE FAITHFULNESS OF GOD
WHEN ALL SEEMS LOST. HOW MIRACLES CAN UNFOLD
IN THE MOST UNLIKELY OF MOMENTS, AND WHAT
GOD CAN DO WHEN WE SAY "YES" TO HIM.

Annette Tuttle

Trilogy Christian Publishers
A Wholly Owned Subsidiary of Trinity Broadcasting Network
2442 Michelle Drive
Tustin, CA 92780

For information, address Trilogy Christian Publishing
Rights Department, 2442 Michelle Drive, Tustin, Ca 92780.
Trilogy Christian Publishing/ TBN and colophon are trademarks of Trinity Broadcasting Network.

For information about special discounts for bulk purchases, please contact Trilogy Christian Publishing.

Manufactured in the United States of America

10 9 8 7 6 5 4 3 2 1

Library of Congress Cataloging-in-Publication Data is available.

ISBN 978-1-64088-919-4 (Print Book)
ISBN 978-1-64088-920-0 (ebook)

To Ken Whitten, founder of Vision International Missions

Ken, you made it possible for me and countless others
to experience the mission field in Haiti and across the
world. Because of your love and unceasing dedication
to the lost, the poor, and the sick, you gave me an
opportunity to have my heart awakened to do the same.

Eye has not seen, nor ear heard,
Nor have entered into the heart of man
The things which God has prepared
for those who love Him.
                    —1 Corinthians 2:9 (NKJV)

To the reader
and to all who have become weary,
disappointed, or feel that all is lost,

God has a plan for your life.
Hold on.
It's just around the corner.

CONTENTS

◆

PREFACE

◆

This story is about so many things, but mainly it's about God: the One who hears and sees us. It's about the God who comes to our rescue when we call upon His name. It's about a God who is a master conductor, symphony orchestrator, and expert chess player—putting all the right pieces together at just the right time. Just when we think all is lost, hold on! God will show up in all of His glory and unfold the beautiful details that become the story of our lives.

I wanted to tell this story for all the lost, broken, fearful, and desperate people who have no hope and feel that all is lost. God has a plan for your life, and He will go to great lengths to meet you right where you are. What He does for one, He will do for another.

What a great joy it has been to write our story. I laughed and cried so many times as I recalled the unfathomable faithfulness of Jesus. The details of how this story all came together are nothing short of miraculous. I pray you are encouraged by all that God has done, but more so, to know that God will do it again in your life too.

I want to thank my beautiful Bulgarian friend Iva, who first encouraged me to write this story down. Thank you for your anointed suggestion. Thank you, Shultz, for lending your voice and giving us a glimpse of your incredible journey from the rubble of Haiti to the soil of America. Thank you,

Laurie Konyalian, for helping pull the writer out of me and keeping me on track. Lastly, I want to thank my husband, Gordon, who has made a way for me over and over again to pursue God with all my heart.

CHAPTER 1

◆

An Unexpected Opportunity

A comfort zone is a beautiful place
but nothing ever grows there.

—Anon

Annette

The snow glistened in hues of icy blue as the sun dipped behind the trees in the distance. The peaceful winter view from my living room was strikingly beautiful. How I loved the safety and security of my home in the winter. Feeling a little chilly from the frigid New Hampshire scenery in front of me, I brewed a cup of hot tea. I then sat down on the sofa and turned on the news. It had been a long and busy day, and I sat to catch my breath. It was Tuesday, January 12, 2010. My attention suddenly focused on a breaking news headline as I saw, "Devastating earthquake, 7.0 on the Richter scale strikes the nation of Haiti." I leaned forward as I continued to watch. The news anchor reported that the epicenter of the earthquake was apparently just outside a town called

Léogâne. I quickly learned that the town of Léogâne was around fifteen miles west of Port-au-Prince, Haiti's capital. The details continued to unfold as the reporter spoke quickly and concisely in front of mounds.

For the next several days, I continued to watch the news updates on the disaster in Haiti. The rising death toll was staggering. As I watched, I saw such suffering and desperation. I knew the Lord wanted to challenge me to step out and do something. As I sat on my living-room couch, I spoke with the Lord in my heart, asking, *Do You want me to go?* As soon as I uttered that prayer, I was flooded with doubt. *What could I possibly do there?* I have no medical training, nothing to bring to the people. *I don't speak the language!* The questions raced in my mind over the rubble. "Thousands of people are estimated to be affected by this earthquake. Many losing their homes, many injured and many dead…" My heart sank. I was shocked at what was being reported. "Haiti is documented to be the poorest country in the Western Hemisphere and was already a nation in crisis before it was impacted by this earthquake," the newscaster continued.

What I saw on television was *everything* but structured, orderly, and comfortable—the complete opposite of my world. For the remaining time of the news segment, all I saw on television was images of rubble, death, chaos, confusion, and destruction. I could feel the weight of the situation, and my heart began to break for the people who were now impacted by this catastrophe. At that moment, although I could not put my finger on it, something began to stir deep within my soul. Over the next few days, I found my emotions in a tug-of-war—a wrestle between compassion and fear. Fear was fighting to dominate my heart and mind. I gave every excuse I could think of not to go to Haiti. I knew that every aspect of clinging to what was comfortable would be challenged in me. At this point in my life, I had already been on a few mission trips, but in many ways, missions was still new to me. I continued to wrestle with the idea of going to Haiti. Would I shrink back, or would I follow through?

By the end of that week, I decided I was going to Haiti, even though my fear was telling me otherwise. Having connections with a missions organization called Vision International Missions, I decided to contact the director, Ken Whitten. Ken Whitten had been to Haiti many, many times before, taking medical mission teams with him. I knew that if anyone was going to help Haiti in the wake of its recent catastrophe, it would be Ken. I decided to call him and learned during the phone conversation that he was already planning to go to Haiti and wanted to take a team with him. As the phone call came to an end, I knew this was my opportunity to go. The team would be a small one and would consist of Ken, Melissa, and myself, along with doctors, a nurse, and a few others.

~~~~

It was February 22, 2010, and I was on my way to Haiti. The seat-belt sign turned on abruptly. A voice spoke quickly yet calmly through the intercom.

"Ladies and gentlemen, we will be landing in Santo Domingo shortly. Please fasten your seat belts and prepare for landing. Thank you for your cooperation."

As I fastened my seat belt, Ken beamed a smile to us on the team. The plan seemed to be unfolding quite smoothly. We knew beforehand that we would land in the Dominican Republic, and then we would go across the border into Haiti in a rented bus. I was excited and anxious at the same time. *What is it like on the other side of the border?* I closed my eyes and tried to imagine what Haiti would be like in real life. Then I said a short prayer as the airplane descended rapidly to land.

~ ~ ~ ~

Hot, long, arduous—these are a few words that accurately describe the next part of the journey. As we exited the airport in Santo Domingo, we headed to a small hotel to eat and sleep for a few hours before heading to the Haitian border. I did not sleep a wink that night because the hotel room was old, musty, and filthy—stretching my comfort zone. At 2:30 a.m., we loaded the bus with our supplies and headed for the border. I had a splitting headache and already felt exhausted, but was relieved to be out of the hotel.

The Haitian border drew nearer as the sun was rising with vivid brilliance. At this point, I knew everything was about to change. I looked out of the window and saw hundreds of people. There was an endless line of cars, buses, and trucks that wanted to get across the border. Many of these trucks were peacekeeping vehicles and different humanitarian organizations that were bringing aid to Haiti. Then all of a sudden, our bus was pulled over, detained, and our bags searched. During the search, my apprehension was at an all-time high. I only had a small backpack with me since most of the luggage space allocated for the team was used to transport medical supplies. *What am I doing here?* The search was time-consuming and nerve-racking.

We finally made it across the border, the heat slowly intensifying as the morning wore on. As we made our way to Port-au-Prince, I was hit with the reality of what was happening in Haiti. The streets we drove by were filled with people. Pollution and small debris particles filled the air in a hazy fog. Rubble was seen everywhere, and the faces of people were somber, exhausted, and desperate. *How am I going to help these people, Lord?* I prayed within my heart.

The air was hot, foul, and putrefying. The smell of human waste hung heavily in the still, humid air, along with the smell of rotting food and garbage. I was shocked and horrified. The putrid smell was so strong that I thought I was going to vomit. As the vehicle traveled down the road, I was amazed to see sights that I had never seen before. Hundreds of people on the streets, collapsed buildings and houses, people walking in a hundred different directions amidst the crazy traffic, sights you simply do not see in New Hampshire. By the time Ken, Melissa, and I and the rest of the team reached the base where we were to stay, all my senses had been bombarded by the heat, sights, smells and sounds from all around. I called my pastor to tell him that the team had arrived safely, and I remember saying, "If there is a hell, this is it!"

As the day wore on, the sun beat down strongly; nothing was hidden from its strength. Everything seemed to languish in the heat. It was easy to become dehydrated. Clean, drinkable water was a high priority for our team. Keeping water bottles full and drinking from small plastic bags became our constant source of hydration. As I took my plastic bag, I saw that it was covered with a film of dust. I didn't care. Parched, I gulped the water down quickly.

Soon it was evening, and I was trying to process all that I had seen that first day. In an effort to cool off, I took a cloth to clean my hot cheeks. By the time I had wiped my face, I was shocked to see that the cloth was as black as soot. It was as though I had just wiped off a sticky film of dirt that the polluted air, along with the heat, had plastered on my face. *What am I doing here?* At that moment, I felt as though I could not cope with what I had experienced that first day in Haiti and wanted the easy way out. I thought I would just take the first flight back home to the United States, and that would be it. As I lay in bed to go to sleep, I cried out to the Lord to help me. My prayer was a simple plea: *Lord, give me grace to stay.* Then I fell into a deep slumber, exhausted.

I woke up the next morning feeling refreshed, knowing that God had answered my prayer. I could feel His grace. As I looked out of the small window in the room I was staying in, I was delighted to see the sun rising. It was as if the light bathed the village with new hope, the crowing of roosters as well as the barking of dogs having woken me up. The early morning sounds of Haiti! Little did I know that the animals in the village would become my morning alarm clock from then on! As I started my day, I no longer felt like I wanted to go back to the security of my life back in America but felt the grace to stay in Haiti and be used by God in any way He saw fit. Contagious joy was now bubbling from within me. I felt a sense of hopeful anticipation as our team prepared for the days ahead. It was not that the situation in Port-au-Prince and the surrounding villages would not be difficult to face, but I knew deep down inside that I would not face it alone. Ken was an experienced team leader. We had medical staff on our team, and most importantly, I knew God was with us.

The hours slipped by quickly. Days passed as we, as a team, continued diligently in our work. By the fourth day, we headed into the mountains outside of Port-au-Prince in a truck to set up a medical clinic. As we sat in the back of the truck, I wore sunglasses to protect my eyes that had become so irritated from debris particles. I also wore a mask over my nose since my throat and lungs were feeling the effects of breathing in the polluted air. Riding in the back of trucks or in a van became a wonderful adventure. The traffic in Port-au-Prince was an experience like nothing I had ever seen. Thousands of cars, motorcycles with many people on them, dangerously overloaded trucks, as well as thousands of people were out on the streets. Cars were seemingly driving in any and all directions, driving at crazy speeds. Drivers using their horns as blinkers only added to the extraordinary noise level. It was a sight to behold! Every road and every curve in the road was an adventure. The ride toward the mountains caused my adrenaline to spike! Were we going to reach our destination safe and sound?

On the way up, the sight of myriads of people trying to deal with the aftermath of the earthquake was overwhelming, and the repercussions were seen everywhere. Tent cities had been set up to provide shelter for thousands of people who had lost their homes. There were no bathrooms, no sanitation, and no running water. Fear of diseases like cholera and typhoid loomed over the people. Hundreds needed water, food, and medical care. My heart was heavy.

Upon arriving to our mountain location, our team quickly set up a medical clinic. The plan for the day was now familiar as our team knew which tasks needed to be done and when. Our team would divide into several sections: The medical team would treat people who were injured or needed care; some set up a pharmacy. Others would hand out clothes, soap, shampoo, and toothpaste. My role was to pray for anyone who wanted prayer, as people came through the line. Soon enough, droves of villagers made their way to the clinic; some of them had injuries that needed immediate attention. *Lord, that is a lot of people, help me! Who will be my interpreter today since I do not know Creole or French?* I wondered how the Lord would provide someone who spoke English and would be willing to spend the day with me.

~~~~

"I heard you are looking for an interpreter," spoke a voice above the clamor of the crowd that was now forming to get medical help.

I turned and saw the face of a young man. He looked about the same age as one of my sons: early twenties. His face was thin but bore an expression of determination. He looked eager to help.

"You speak English!" I responded.

I was shocked and relieved at the same time.

"Yes, they told me there was need here for translation into English, so I got here as fast as I could. I am here to help," said the young man.

He seemed worn out but determined. I quickly learned that his name was D'Meza Shultz Pierre Louis, or *Shultz* for short. Shultz was to be the answer to my prayer!

"Shultz," I asked, "could you stay with me today and interpret as I pray for people?"

It was day four, and God had finally brought an interpreter my way! An interpreter who could translate my English into Creole so that people could understand what I was praying. I was relieved and felt like there was a breakthrough that day as Shultz and I prayed and ministered to hundreds of people. The openness and hunger for prayer was evident in the people who came through the line. Many in despair, many full of fear and worry, many needing physical healing. But regardless of why people came, God met every one of them. Hearts were hungering for the Living God! For the first time since my arrival in Haiti, I saw how God was using my simple, childlike prayers to plant small seeds of hope into fragile, frightened hearts.

What first appeared as a chance meeting of two people or *happenstance*, was in fact the beginning of how two lives would be changed forever. Who knew how the course of subsequent events would unfold? The reason as to why God had sent me to Haiti was now slowly being unraveled before my very eyes.

CHAPTER 2

◆

In Thirty-Two Seconds

I searched for a faint, flickering light,
One that would dispel
The deep and heavy night.
—Laurie Konyalian

Therefore, we will not fear, even though the
earth be removed and though the mountains
be carried into the midst of the sea.
—Psalm 46:2 (NJKV)

Shultz

It was a day like any other day at Sogebank, at the bank where
I, D'Meza Shultz Pierre Louis, worked as a market researcher.
Having completed my work tasks for the day, I decided to
stop by the university to see some of my college friends at
the Faculté de Droit et des Sciences Economiques, or the
Faculty of Law and Economics. It was late afternoon, and
my friends were getting ready for their college graduation

ceremony as they completed the last class project for their program. I walked calmly yet quickly for about one mile to a bustling intersection called Portail Léogâne, or *Pòtay Leyogàn* in Creole. Crammed with people, it was common to see a flurry of activity at Portail Léogâne. Various farm goods such as sugarcane, mangoes, plantains, and the like were sold here.

"Fresh mangoes, fresh mangoes for sale," cried a merchant of fruits, trying to sell his produce.

The scent of luscious mangoes filled the warm air as people rushed through the lively streets. It was at this intersection where I usually waited for a tap-tap—a bus or a truck that served as a taxi. Soon enough, I hopped on the ornately decorated tap-tap that would take me close to home.

It was 4:53 p.m. Half a mile down the highway, the tap-tap started to shake violently. I looked around to see people screaming frantically at the top of their lungs. What was going on? My eyes widened in shock as I realized that not only was the bus collapsing, but whole concrete buildings were swaying as the ground shook. Within thirty-two seconds, all the buildings around me had collapsed, and bodies were trapped under the rubble. Loud piercing cries filled the air as bloody bodies wailed in shock. My thoughts were racing. Were we being bombed? It was as if time stood still. A nightmare had unfolded before my eyes. I was now in what appeared to be a war zone.

I started running as fast as I could. The ground trembled so intensely that I wanted to fly, if that were possible, and stay in midair. I started to take bigger leaps to try to avoid absorbing the shock of the continued tremors. *This must be an earthquake. Is Mom okay? How about my sister, Anonde, and Uncle Yves?* I desperately held back tears as I tried to quickly call home on my cell phone. There was no connection. In a state of panic, I decided to run to my half sister's house to see if everyone was okay there and then made my way back home. On my way, I saw cars and gas stations lit on fire with unrelenting flames that were spreading uncontrollably. People were running in all directions as utter chaos broke loose. I continued to run, trying to stay in the middle of the road to avoid crumbling buildings. I was desperate. *Will I get home alive? WILL I, WILL I?* I screamed within myself.

As I turned the corner onto my street, not only was my blood racing, but my mind was racing as well. I felt nauseous and shocked that I was still actually alive. I was relieved to see that my mom, sister, and uncle were alive. We clung to one another and cried intensely for several minutes with the overwhelming sentiment of both shock and relief all at the same time. I was relieved to learn that many of our neighbors had also survived the earthquake. In the days that followed, telephone connections were no longer working, and communication was limited. The already inferior roads were now impassable. We heard rumors that trucks were transporting dead bodies to a large dump about one hundred miles away from the borough I lived in. As the days passed, the grief and pain became unbearable. Continual reports concerning those who died, those who were injured, those who were homeless were more than we could bear. No one was left untouched by the misery of what was now daily life in Haiti. Some of my friends from school and church did not survive, and every day became a day of mourning. Every day brought more news of suffering and heartbreak.

It is one matter to believe that God exists, and it is an entirely different matter to believe that God is in control. Faith in the latter was sometimes a struggle for me, not only after the earthquake but before it as well. Before Haiti was hit by the quake, the country already ranked among the most impoverished nations in the Western Hemisphere. Haiti also ranked the fifteenth most corrupt country in the world. These facts not only impacted the nation but also had a ripple effect on the way my family and I lived our lives. Work was hard to come by. Food was often scarce; the main food we ate was rice and beans. Drought was a constant reality. Our main source of water came from rainwater, which we collected from the rooftops. We were stricken by hunger and thirst and want. Sickness and violence was our dreaded yet familiar companion.

I was born on the same day that Haitian history books record as the start of democracy in the nation. February 7, 1986, was the day that ended the decades-long oppressive regime of President Jean-Claude Duvalier. My grandmother's rendition of the story of my birth has it that weeks before I was born, an unknown doula visited my grandmother's house. The doula emphatically stated that she was sent there to ensure that I was born safely and did not leave the house until I was born. Once I was born, the mysterious doula left my mother's side and was seen no more.

I was raised by my mother, who was a single mom. My mom gave of herself selflessly every day so that her children could survive. Although my mom could not read or write, she strongly believed in getting an education. It was my mom's wish that her children would complete high school and get a diploma.

During my high school years, I played soccer as an extracurricular activity and was part of the school drama club. Occasionally, I also shared on Sunday mornings at the church where I attended. After high school, I continued acting since I enjoyed it, and it helped me pay the bills to support my family. Coincidentally, at that time, I met the ex-president of Haiti, Michele Duvivier Pierre Louis, who was also the founder of a foundation called Fokal. Outside of my family, it was Michele Duvivier Pierre Louis who supported me financially through the Fokal foundation as she saw my potential and my diligence in academic performance. In addition to this, I was a member of a theater company called Dram'Art. We toured Haiti and played in the Festival des Quatre-Chemins, which was sponsored by the Fokal foundation. Later on, I founded my own one-man theater company where I had the chance to perform and tour. These were valuable opportunities to make a few dollars, enough to carry me and my family forward on our quest of daily survival.

After I completed high school, my family could not afford to send me to university. To add to this, there was a lot of competition for students to get accepted into the main public university. Getting accepted into this university was difficult because there were too many applicants and also because rich families would bribe college officials to get their children accepted into university. This made my chance to get a college education even more slim. Despite all odds, I got accepted into two major programs at the university— the School of Engineering and the School of Economics and Law. I chose to go with the School of Economics and Law. The opportunity to go to university and study a major I enjoyed was a miracle in and of itself!

As a Christian family with a strong faith, my family and I believed and trusted in God for everything we needed for daily life. After the earthquake, however, everything changed for the worse. We were hit by the reality that life was about to get much more difficult. I was twenty-four years old when the earthquake hit and shook my life down to its core, causing its very foundations to tremble. I always thought that I would graduate from university, work as a financier in either the public or private sector, but that seemed impossible now.

The earthquake had put an end to my aspirations. After the earthquake, all that I knew and all that I had worked for was gone, like useless chaff that is thrown to the wind.

In the aftermath of this disaster, anger surged within my soul. I could not bottle it in any longer; my anger was like waves of the ocean that could not be restrained. Being the oldest child, I had provided for my family, bringing home the finances for rent, school, food, and daily living. *What am I going to do now?* I was completely baffled. Our home was destroyed, the bank for which I worked was in ruins, and my job was lost. My college and the church where I attended had collapsed. Everything had crumbled into nothing in thirty-two seconds.

In my devastation, I began to direct my anger at God and began to doubt that He was really in control. If He was indeed a good God, how could He let this disaster happen, after all that we had already suffered as a nation?

The questions lingered as my mom, sister, uncle, and I spent many sleepless nights on the streets. The faintest of sounds in the night had us running in fear that another earthquake was imminent. As the days wore on, the questions continued to rage in my mind. *What is God trying to prove? Is He trying to crush a people who are already suffering?* Sleeplessly, I clenched my jaw and grit my teeth as I stared into the dark night.

News quickly spread throughout the country that there was a fleet of US Navy ships stationed at the seaport and that translators were in high demand by the first responding soldiers. As resources became more and more scarce, I decided to go to the seaport to see if I could get a job as a translator. Eager to find work, I woke up around 4:00 a.m. to get to the seaport before the gates opened. I thought that if I was there early, I would have a greater chance to talk to an officer who was hiring for translation jobs. Optimism arose in my heart to think that maybe, just maybe, all my effort to learn English would finally pay off.

Just before the port gates opened each morning, crowds of people would wait at the gate in hopes of getting in. As the time of the opening of the gates drew near, droves of people pressed on every side, trying to squeeze their way closer to the gate. The commotion of the crowd was noisy and almost deafening. The yelling and pushing of multitudes rang out with an air of intense desperation. Everyone wanted to be hired. By the time I got through the gate and was a few feet from the soldiers in charge of hiring, I was exhausted. The résumé in my hand, which I held on to so tightly, was crumpled and sweaty. In that moment, it felt as though my whole life depended on that résumé.

Disappointment soon followed, as no one wanted to look at or even take my résumé. I continued to go back to the port day after day, rising early in the morning each time, hoping I would get a job as a translator. Each day I went away empty-handed. I had multiple résumés at hand, ready for the first employer that would hire me. Having almost completed a degree in economics and having the flexibility to speak English, Spanish, French, and Creole, I thought I would get a job straight away. Days passed, and still there was no job for me. My hopes were sinking. I was exhausted just trying to find a simple job. Sleeping on the streets every night did not help the situation at all as the night air had become toxic, now saturated with the stench of rotting corpses. As the days rolled on, my health became fragile. I was gaunt, underweight, and coughing up blood. My mom watched helplessly as my health suffered.

One day, a friend of mine randomly told me about Oxfam GB, a nonprofit organization which had been on the ground in Haiti since 1978. Apparently, this organization was in dire need of interpreters. Without wasting any time, I decided to go to the organization, taking several résumés with me. Oxfam GB was located on the north end, the richer side of Port-au-Prince, in a place called Pétion-ville. I used whatever money I had left for transportation and was left to walk the rest of the way there. It was also the first time that I was scared of being shot, as it was common to get shot in that area if you were traveling on foot. I was terrified.

I finally reached my destination. On one of the walls of the building, there was more information about the job and the kind of candidates the organization was looking for. After knocking on a tall red iron gate, a large, burly man with a twelve-gauge shotgun opened a window to address me. His demeanor was cold and stoic.

"Why have you come?" asked the security guard sternly.

I pushed several résumés toward the window, believing this was my chance.

"Sorry, sir, I cannot let you in. We are not hiring anymore. Interviews are finished for the day," said the guard with a sly half smile on his face.

Maybe they really aren't hiring anymore. I was trying to console myself. Several minutes later, the same guard was taking résumés from other people who were behind me in the lineup. *Maybe bribes are involved? Or maybe they are family and friends of the security guard?* Who knew and who cared? This was the reality in Haiti! Devastated, I left with no more money in my wallet.

As I walked home, I cried. The weight of trying to help my family survive financially felt like a burden I could no longer carry. All I wanted was a simple job to help me pay for the necessities of life. Absorbed in deep thought, I lost my way. I was lost, totally lost, and frankly, I did not care. I cried and shouted at God with a loud voice.

"YOU DON'T CARE AT ALL!" I yelled. I was fuming with anger. "How are your promises true? HOW! JUST TELL ME HOW!" I bellowed.

There comes a time in life when not only *what* you believe in but *whom* you believe in must be called upon. For the majority in Haiti, this was witchcraft; but for me, it was Jesus Christ. Growing up, however, I became curious to read about different faiths. My curiosity ranged from Islam, Hinduism, Catholicism, Judaism, and Jehovah's Witnesses. By the time, the earthquake had hit the country. I believed in Jesus as my Lord and Savior and that if I did the right thing, He would show His goodness to me. I had worked hard and earned money and was almost finished my schooling at a public university. But now it seemed like everything I had been working for was crumbling into piles of rubble. *What has my life come to? What is going to happen to me and my family? Has God passed us by?* I was angry and did not understand why all of this had happened. *There are bigger issues in the world—God isn't interested in my troubles.*

As I wandered through the streets, people heard me yelling and surely thought I was out of my mind. People who were passing by were not moved by the sight of a man yelling in the streets. It was quite common to see people who had lost all soundness of mind walking around town. At one point, lifting up my arms and looking to the sky, I begged God to take my résumé and do whatever He wanted with it. I wanted God to prove Himself to me and show me in a tangible way that He existed; that He was in control, and that He cared. Several weeks had already passed, and still I could not find a job. I was at the end of myself. Either God was to come through, or I felt like I would die. I was at a crossroad—either God would show up, or I no longer had faith in Him. As I gathered my thoughts to find my way home, I heard the honking of a car behind me. I looked around and saw a white pickup truck with the Oxfam GB logo on it. I slowly approached the truck. As I took a closer look, the driver looked as though he wanted to talk to me.

"Hello, Shultz! *Is that you?*" said the man.

It was as if this man had seen me around before. As I took a closer look at the man's face, I was surprised! It was someone I knew from my college.

"Mr. DuBien! What brings you here?" I asked.

"Oh, I am working for Oxfam GB now!" Mr. DuBien answered, his eyes beaming with hope.

"I was trying to get an interview for a potential job at Oxfam GB," I explained.

"I heard you screaming from over there and wondered what brought you to this area," Mr. DuBien continued, pointing to the bend in the road a little way up. "I could take a few of your résumés to Oxfam, son," said Mr. DuBien with a kind smile.

My jaw dropped as Mr. DuBien said those words. My heart was racing. *Did God just hear my cry?* A few minutes ago, I was shouting at God and had given Him a deadline; and now I was speaking with Mr. DuBien, who worked for Oxfam GB. I was so shocked that I began to tremble. I raised my hands, asked God to forgive me, and thanked Him for coming through for me when I least expected it. At that moment, I also felt a sense of shame for shouting at God, and I began to cry. Mr. DuBien waited there in total silence for a minute or so and then spoke up. He had a twinkle in his eye.

"The light always dispels the night, Shultz. Hold on to hope, son."

And at that, he drove off. I could not believe what I had just heard! I thought God had forgotten me, but from one moment to the next, everything changed. God had stepped into my reality to show me in a tangible way that He truly cared for me. At that moment, I was reassured that God was able to get me a job and that nothing was too difficult for Him!

I walked as fast as I could to tell my mom, sister, and uncle Yves all that had happened that afternoon.

"This is great news!" said Uncle Yves.

"What an answer to prayer! We should have never doubted!" exclaimed Anonde.

"This is reason to celebrate Poupon!" said my mom. "God is sovereign but always good and should never be questioned," continued my mom with a big grin.

Little did I know that the story had only just begun! My mom began to tell me that she just received a call from my aunt Arianne, who lived in the mountains in the next town. Apparently, there was news that American missionaries were coming to Haiti to provide medical assistance to the people in the villages.

"I think you should go with me to meet these missionaries, Shultz. You could get some medication for your poor health, and I can hear you speak some English!" said my mom, who had not heard me speak in English before.

It seemed like a good plan. I would get some medicine since I had a fever and I could practice my English.

The next morning, I made every excuse in my mind not to go to meet the missionaries. Nevertheless, my mom and I rose early and made our way to a town called Merger, which was where my aunt Josette lived. Merger was a small town twelve miles south of the nation's capital in between Port-au-Prince and Léogâne. Little did I know that going to my aunt's house that day would change my life forever.

At my aunt Josette's house, which was on top of a hill, there was a temporary medical clinic set up. The clinic attracted a long line of people who wanted to get medical help. Since my mom and I had arrived at the house early, I quickly received the medical attention I needed, and my mom and I went through another line that was handing out basic necessities like soap, t-shirts, and sandals. I was relieved to receive some basic toiletry items. I smelled the soap and smiled. *The sheer scent of freshness!* I thought to myself, both comforted and relieved.

Later I found out that two of the missionaries were named Annette and Melissa. Annette and Melissa were at the fourth station praying for people. They prayed with gentleness and asked people if they knew Jesus Christ as their Savior. Annette realized that I spoke English, and she asked if I would be interested in staying with her for the day to translate her prayers for people. I agreed to help. I was happy to speak English for the very first time with Americans! That day was truly a life-transforming day for me! Praying for people encouraged my faith, made me feel closer to God, and gave me a new boldness to share my faith in Jesus Christ with others. This was a new reality to live in for me, as before I felt that I was too frail in my faith to carry the weight of sharing the Good News with others. But that day was a turning point for me—not only in encouraging me in my faith but also in catapulting me further into the plan that God had for my life.

CHAPTER 3

◆

The Path Less Traveled

Two roads diverged in a wood, and I—
I took the one less traveled by,
And that has made all the difference.

—Robert Frost

Annette

As the sun began to blaze and the heat of the day intensified, the lineup of people wanting prayer dwindled. I now had a chance to listen to Shultz's story.

"I have lost everything," said Shultz, his brow furrowing deeply. "My home, my church, my college, my job at the bank—all gone."

As I heard the details of all that had happened to Shultz and his family, my heart began to break for this precious young man. The scope of the devastation and the sheer hopelessness of what was ahead for him troubled me. *What if one of my sons had lost everything in one day like Shultz had?*

With the last of the villagers receiving medical care, it was time for our team to say goodbye to all the precious people we had met. Giving a final hug to everyone, I felt deeply emotional. Leaving and saying goodbye was more difficult than I thought it would be.

"You take care of yourself, Shultz," I said one last time as I gathered my things and headed toward the van.

"You as well, Annette," replied Shultz.

As the van jolted its way down the rugged mountain road to take our team back to our base, I turned back to look one last time at all the people I had met. They were waving at the van in gratitude, their smiling faces slowly fading into the distance. Sadness flooded my heart because I was sure I would never see these people or Shultz ever again.

That day in the mountains of Haiti, for the first time ever, I understood the scope of what it meant to me to be an American citizen. For me, it was like a line of demarcation. Below the line was survival: people who barely made ends meet; their vision in life was consumed by meeting the demands of everyday living, such as having food, water, shelter, and safety. Above the line, on the other hand, was where individuals did not just survive, but they had the chance to dream, have hopes and aspirations. Living above the line meant having the chance to thrive—get an education and succeed. My sons were living "above the line." They lived in the daily realization that they could accomplish anything they wanted to accomplish, attain any profession they wanted to attain, and become anything they wanted to be. Not once did my sons ever wonder whether they would eat or drink on any given day, or if they would have a place to lay their heads at night. Education was a must in our house: my sons would go to college and study what they wanted to study. At the same time I met Shultz, my son Phil was working so hard to fulfill his dream to be a professional soccer player, and my son Chris was on track to becoming a lawyer. Both of my boys were positioned to live out their dreams. My sons were truly sons of privilege, not because we were rich, because we were not, but simply because we had choices and opportunities. I wanted that for Shultz. As a mother of two sons, I wanted Shultz to have the opportunity to thrive.

Shultz had so many dreams and aspirations, but now they were all gone. What Shultz had accomplished in his life up until the earthquake, and what he was still hoping for, was destroyed in a pile of rubble. Were Shultz to stay in Haiti, he would once again be living below the line—living a life of survival. I knew right then and there that I could not leave Shultz in Haiti. Shultz seemed too intelligent and too talented to stay there. He deserved a better life, one where there are more open doors of opportunity.

Maybe Shultz should come to the United States? Is that even a possibility?

After returning home to New Hampshire, there was not a day that passed by where I did not think about Shultz and prayed for his safety. I prayed for direction and for God's will to be done in Shultz's life.

~ ~ ~

I looked out the paned window in the living room. It had rained earlier that day, and flowers with new buds were now basking in the warm afternoon light. Spring was in bloom. Absorbed in thought, I turned and took another sip of my tea. The soothing aroma of mint tea filled the air. I thought it was time I spoke to my husband about my recent reflections.

"I really think Shultz should come to the United States," I said with conviction.

My husband was reading a newspaper, his head buried in the headlines of the day.

"What do you think?" I asked.

My husband looked up. Then putting the paper away, he focused on what I was saying.

I continued to speak. "He could finish his undergraduate degree here in America," I added.

My husband listened attentively. "He could definitely have more opportunity here, that is for sure," my husband concurred.

"Opportunities that Phil and Chris have," I replied

The conversation continued. After much discussion and prayer, my husband and I unanimously decided to begin the process of bringing Shultz to America. We were about to walk along a path we had never traveled before—a path that would require unwavering courage and determination. The path less traveled.

As we began the process, so many questions were running through my mind. *God, are You in this? Where do we begin? Is this even possible?* My constant prayer was, *Lord, lead us!*

Bringing Shultz to the United States was going to be a challenge, especially navigating through a country that lay in ruins. We would have to navigate the student visa process for a Haitian to attend an American university, obtain a passport, medical records, college transcripts, in addition to endless forms and documents. Every day, I prayed the same prayer: *God, if You're not in this, close the doors.* Knowing the impossible mountain I was up against, I fully expected doors to close at every junction; but to my surprise, the doors kept opening, one after another.

~~~~

"Do I have an appointment with you?" said Mr. LeBlanc, the president of Southern New Hampshire University, walking out his office.

"I believe so," I answered calmly.

"I have another appointment shortly, but I can give you about five minutes," confirmed the president.

My husband and I looked at each other, both surprised and relieved. We knew we had scheduled an appointment with the president of the college, but it seemed it was not on his appointment calendar. Nevertheless, this was the moment we were waiting for! *I had five minutes.* I took the picture of Shultz and myself that we had taken the day we met and handed it to the president.

"Mr. LeBlanc, I met this young man in February while on a mission trip to Haiti. Due to the earthquake, he has lost everything. Do you think that you could give him to scholarship and bring him here to finish his degree?"

Mr. LeBlanc leaned back in his chair, pondered for what seemed like an eternity, then looked at us.

"Yes, I think we could do that," he replied.

My husband and I were in complete shock and disbelief at what we had just heard. God had opened a big door wide open.

"If you raise the money for his room and board, we will pay for his tuition," Mr. LeBlanc continued.

Shultz had just received a scholarship to come to America! On that rainy April day, as my husband and I left the president's office, we were in awe of this God story that we found ourselves a part of. Was this really happening? Shultz was indeed coming to America! The following day, I received an official e-mail from the president of the college stating that the university would pay for Shultz to complete a degree.

~ ~ ~

Shultz

In was April in Haiti, and the roads had still not been cleared from all the rubble, and Port-au-Prince was congested with people. In the hustle and bustle of the inner city, I kept bumping into passersby who, like myself, were at the central marketplace called Marché Hyppolite. There was a frantic rush in the marketplace as people were buying whatever food they could find. As I was about to buy some plantains, my cell phone rang. I answered quickly and was surprised to find out that it was a call from the United States.

"Shultz, it's Annette from America. Can you hear me?"

The phone connection was crackling, and it was difficult to hear what was being said on the other end of the line. But I managed to pick up bits and pieces from what Annette was saying.

"Shultz, I have news for you," continued Annette, speaking with a louder volume, hoping to be heard more clearly. "You just got a scholarship. You're coming to America to finish school."

Is this a joke? Is Annette joking?

"Annette, are you telling me the truth? Please do not lie to me, American lady!" I replied.

"Shultz, I'm telling you the truth. You're coming to America," replied Annette.

Growing up in Haiti, I was used to empty promises, so I was not sure if Annette was really telling me the truth or not.

"Shultz, I am not kidding you, this is real. You really can come to the United States and study!" Annette continued, trying to reassure me.

I was both astonished and nervous. It was a lot to take in all at once!

That same day, I received an e-mail from Annette stating that all she said on the phone earlier was the truth. The way had opened for me to go to the United States—I could hardly believe it! Upon learning that I had received a scholarship to go to America to study, I could hardly contain my joy; it felt like I was bursting at the seams! The news was really good news, almost too good to be true! I told my very close family, but unfortunately some of my closest friends had to be left in the dark. This was because people in Haiti do not share their advancement or success in fear that others may become jealous of them in their progress. There is this looming mind-set of fear over the nation that someone may just try to thwart your plans if they are good and are leading you toward abundance or blessing.

Several days after that, Annette forwarded the letter from the president of Southern New Hampshire University showing I had been given a scholarship to finish my undergraduate degree. I was in awe of how God would send Annette across thousands of miles, all the way to Haiti, to be an agent of hope. God was about to literally airlift me out of my circumstance.

CHAPTER 4

◆

The Paper Chase

By my God I can leap over a wall.
—Psalm 18:29 (NKJV)

Annette

Sometimes, I think it is better to not know the height of the mountain you are about to scale before you endeavor to scale it. I had no idea what lay ahead, in terms of all the paperwork that needed to be done in order to bring Shultz to the United States. Little did I know of the obstacles I would face and the hurdles I needed to jump over in order to process the needed documents. All I knew was that I wanted to see Shultz get out of Haiti—and this became my constant motivation. My simple faith helped me greatly, and so did my naivety. In hindsight, I can now see how not knowing the amount of paperwork that was ahead of me was to my benefit

It was still the month of April and the beginning of what seemed like an endless paper chase! The tasks at hand included compiling college transcripts from Haiti, getting Shultz's medical records for both US Immigration and Southern New Hampshire University, getting a student visa for Shultz to stay in the United States, and a passport. All of this had to be accomplished while keeping in mind that Haiti was a third world country that had just collapsed in ruins! Over the next several months, I worked diligently and persistently since the first day of the fall semester at Southern New Hampshire University was only five months away.

~ ~ ~

"International Admissions Office, how may I help you?" asked the voice at the other end of the line.

"May I speak to the Admissions director please?" I replied.

"Just a moment please," replied the operator.

"Hello, this is Connie. How can I help you?"

"Connie? *Connie, is that you?* This is Annette Tuttle," I explained.

"Annette?"

"Yes, it's me. How are you? I can't believe you are still there. How have you been, Connie?" I asked, rather exuberantly.

Over twenty-five years ago, I had worked at Southern New Hampshire University, and Connie was an old coworker of mine. I couldn't believe my ears that she was still working at the college all these years later and was now the associate director of International Admissions! What a comforting turn of events! My heart was completely overwhelmed as I realized that, once again, God was opening wide the door for Shultz to come to the United States! As we continued to converse on the telephone, I took a few minutes to tell Connie the story of Shultz and how President LeBlanc, the president of the university, had agreed to give Shultz a scholarship to finish his undergraduate studies in New Hampshire in the fall.

"Connie, what do I have to do to get Schulz registered for school?" I asked.

"You are asking the right questions!" replied Connie encouragingly.

"This seems to be quite the challenge. Is it going to be possible to request university records from a nation that is under rubble?" I questioned.

"There is a way!" answered Connie with hope.

"Please tell me how," I entreated.

For the next ten minutes, Connie explained the full procedure of how to process Shultz's paperwork.

"That sounds like a plan I can follow!" I concluded.

"Let me know how else I can help you," added Connie.

I felt reassured knowing that Connie was there to help and support me in this paper chase! For the next few minutes, Connie and I chatted like old friends and had a small reunion on the phone. Not only was God continuing to open more doors, but I now had an advocate for the paperwork process in the Office of International Admissions. The path less traveled was a challenging one, but along the way, there were pleasant surprises, such as crossing paths with old friends! Connie was instrumental in helping with the procedure of requesting and processing Shultz's university transcripts. She worked with careful diligence over several months to help me complete the admissions process. This took a load off my shoulders and made things so much easier for me. I am truly grateful for how the Lord orchestrated every detail of the journey, showing me over and over again who He really is and what He is able to do!

~ ~ ~

In addition to navigating the admissions process, I needed to find Shultz a place to live and raise enough money to meet his daily living expenses. The fund-raising process was an extensive one. I started a letter-writing campaign and shared Shultz's story with as many people as possible. I explained what Shultz's monthly expenses were going to be and asked individuals if they would be willing to make monthly donations for about a year. A large number of people started supporting Shultz financially. Through the fund-raising campaign, I raised enough money to pay for Shultz's room, food, transportation, and the clothes he needed for the entire academic year. People faithfully kept their donation pledges, and Shultz was fully supported for the course of the entire upcoming academic year! The doors remained wide open.

In May of 2010, a few months after meeting Shultz, I decided I would go back to Haiti on a mission trip with a team from my church. When the team and I arrived in Haiti, Shultz's met our team at the airport. I was so happy to see him and very grateful to be in Haiti again! As my second visit to Haiti unfolded, I had the opportunity to spend more time with Shultz and his relatives. As I did, the decision to bring Shultz to America was further solidified in my heart. I was confident that I had made the right decision, and I knew that God's fingerprints were all over it. My decision to continue in the process of bringing Shultz to the United States was also confirmed by others on the missions team. This was a relief and a source of great peace and joy. I knew I was on the right path with this decision.

As late spring rolled around, plans for Shultz's arrival were falling into place. Both my husband and I were shocked and so pleased that the International Admissions Office had felt that Shultz had completed all the requirements for an undergraduate degree already, and therefore, they accepted him into the MBA program at Southern New Hampshire University. Having the chance to complete a master of business administration was one of Shultz's dreams—and now it was coming to pass. Everything was coming together; I could hardly believe it. Shultz was coming! Shultz was coming to America, the land of opportunity!

CHAPTER 5

◆

Airlift

No borders, just horizons—only freedom.
—Amelia Earhart

Shultz

I looked outside the small window next to me, and all I could
see were a few wispy white clouds and an endless horizon.
The sky was such a piercing shade of blue that I wanted to
drink in its intensity, if that were possible. At an altitude of
over thirty-five thousand feet, a deep joy was whelming up in
my soul. Sitting right next to the window, I was eager to get
a glimpse of the view. With the earth now out of sight, I felt
so free. It was as though I was in free-fall motion!

This was my first time out of Haiti and my first time
flying in an airplane. After taking in the view for a minute or
so, I picked up my passport: the image of Haitian coat of arms
on the front cover shimmered in the light that streamed from
the window. Running my fingers slowly over the letters that
were embossed in silver, I reread the title quietly in French,

"Republique D'Haiti Passport." I still could not believe that I had a passport! This booklet was like a precious jewel to me. Images flashed through my mind as I remembered the laborious process I had to go through to get my passport: waking up early for about a week and camping outside the immigration and emigration office, where a queue started to form at 4:00 a.m. Thousands of people waited to try to get into the building just to get a passport, and only two hundred people were allowed into the governmental office per day. It was a lengthy process that sucked so much energy out of me but was well worth the toil. It was August 23, 2010, and I was airborne! I could hardly believe that I was on my way to America!

For the longest time that I could remember, no country fascinated me more than the United States of America. As a child, I remember seeing high-flying airplanes overhead in the sky from my grandmother's farm in La Gonâve. Every time I saw airplanes, I would think, *Man, I don't think I would ever have a single shot at being in one of those planes!* At the same time, I always believed God had a big plan for my life. For a lot of people, going to America was not a big deal; but for me, it was the miracle of a lifetime. God was airlifting me out of my circumstance! I was slowly beginning to believe that what lay ahead was better than all that I was leaving behind.

The night before my flight out of Haiti, I did not sleep a wink. I was now hours away from a decision I had made that would alter the course of my life forever. Being someone who always attempted to plan for the unknown, I started to think of all the things that could go wrong on my journey to America. *What if Toussaint Louverture International Airport is closed? What if I get shot by a stray bullet on my way to the airport? What if someone in my extended family suddenly becomes ill and causes my flight to be canceled or postponed?* The questions continued. All I really knew was that I had a student visa which would permit me to study in America for a period of two years. At the same time, I kept hearing a voice at the back of my mind that my training in America would be for a longer period of time, but I had no way of knowing that for sure. I had to come to terms with the fact that I was about to leave my country and had no control over all the unknowns and the what-ifs. I had to let go and just embark on the journey.

The day of my trip to America, I woke up extra early. That morning, my uncle Yves, my sister, and my mom drove me to the airport. My mom was genuinely overjoyed with the door of opportunity that had opened up for me to go to New Hampshire. I had only seen my mom happy two other times in my life: one was when I graduated from high school, and the other was when I was accepted into university in Haiti. My mom was thrilled for me because she was convinced that my potential would quadruple if I left Haiti. Throughout the years, she would often say that I could go anywhere as long as I did not stay in Haiti.

Soon enough, the airplane landed in Miami, Florida. I was in awe by the sight of the airport—it was huge! I was pleased that Annette had booked a flight that had a three-hour layover since it gave me the chance to explore. The airport was teeming with activity and movement. Amused by the hustle and bustle, I noticed that some passengers rushed from one side of the airport to the other. *Maybe they are catching another flight?* Other passengers came out of the Duty Free shop with goods and gifts. *What are they buying?* I was intrigued. As I walked further, the scent of freshly brewed coffee filled the air. Some sat peacefully with a newspaper and a coffee, hoping that time would pass quickly. As I walked around the airport, I let myself get distracted by the large screens that displayed flight information and tried to understand their efficiency and usefulness. I was shocked by how clean and organized everything was. It seemed as though nothing was out of place, yet the airport was an energetic hub of endless activity!

This was my first time in an airport and in a foreign country, and it took me almost three hours to find my way around since my boarding pass had no gate number written on it. The entire experience was so exhilarating that I forgot how hungry I was!

~~~~

"Hello, Annette? It's Shultz!"

"Hi, Shultz! Where are you now?"

The telephone line was so clear.

"I am in the Miami airport!"

"Is everything going okay, Shultz?"

"Yes, everything is fine, Annette."

"That is great to hear, Shultz!"

"I guess I will see you soon, Annette!"

"Yes, take care of yourself and see you soon!"

I hung up quickly. I had promised Annette that I would call her during my stopover to let her know how I was doing. Annette seemed relieved to hear from me, and I was happy to touch base with her. It felt surreal—I had left Haiti and was now in America! I could hardly wait to see Annette again and to meet her husband, Gordon!

The morning before I left Haiti, my aunt Clemene stopped by to say goodbye and brought me some plantains with meat. Several weeks prior to that, I took a trip to La Gonâve Island to say goodbye to my sweet grandma Andrelia. It was difficult to say goodbye to my extended family. The moments were a mixture of both bitter and sweet: bitter because I did not know when I would be back to Haiti, sweet because the land of opportunity was opening up for me.

At Toussaint Louverture International Airport, my mom, uncle, and sister exchanged long hugs as my mom gave me advice on how I should always wear a long sleeved shirt to protect my chest from the brutal New England cold; and how she thought I should behave once I get there. This made my sister giggle! My sister was also happy for me, but both of us knew that our lives would never be the same. Uncle Yves, on the other hand, gave a firm handshake, wished me luck, then humorously told me to avoid doing anything stupid once in America. As I continued to head toward security, my mom wanted to drag my carry-on inside the airport, but the security officer would not let her. I continued on by myself. My family waved at me one final time before they could see me no more.

By the time I landed at the Logan International Airport in Boston, Massachusetts, I had mixed emotions. I felt pure joy, but it was mixed with guilt. How did I end up in America? And why did God choose me out of everyone else in my family? I was still processing the deaths of my friends back in Haiti and had continuous flashbacks of the destruction and horror of the earthquake that I lived through. I was shocked that I was now in America. I never imagined in my wildest dreams that I would ever find myself there.

~ ~ ~ ~

Annette

It was August 23, 2010, a hot summer's day. My husband, Gordon, and I were thrilled that at last this day was upon us. Several months of hard work had finally paid off and Shultz was on his way to America!

As we made our way to the arrivals terminal at Logan International Airport in Boston, Massachusetts, I had a deep realization of the goodness of God and how faithful He is to accomplish His purposes. Even though this day had been long awaited for on our end, I couldn't help but wonder what it was like for Shultz's mother, sister, and family. As my husband and I were about to receive Shultz and welcome him into our lives, Shultz's family had to say goodbye to him and let him go. My heart was so heavy for Shultz and his mom. What was Shultz thinking as he left Haiti? Had he made the right decision to leave his family and come to America? What was it like for Shultz's mom to say goodbye to her only son, not knowing when she would see him again? Saying goodbye must have been heartbreaking. I kept wondering how I would feel if I were to say goodbye to one of my sons, without knowing when I would see him again. My heart was in a state of conflict. On one hand, I was so happy to receive Shultz; but on the other hand, I felt deeply sad that Shultz's family had to let Shultz go, not knowing when he would be back in Haiti.

Knowing that Shultz had never traveled, never been out of Haiti before, and had never been on a plane before made me feel somewhat anxious. *How will he know what to do? Will people be there to help him?* My mother's heart was in full gear as I was so concerned for his safety. *Will he arrive safely?* Throughout the day, we exchanged a short phone call as he made his way to New Hampshire.

We waited impatiently for Shultz at the arrivals terminal, watching to see when he would come through the gate. For everyone who walked through, my first thought was, *is that Shultz?* Finally, after droves of people rushed through the doors, the moment had arrived, Shultz finally came through! My husband and I were relieved. Both of us hugged Shultz, and the three of us laughed and cried all at the same time.

"You are finally here, Shultz!" I exclaimed.

"We are so happy you are here, safe and sound!" said Gordon.

"Let's go get your luggage, Shultz," I said.

"This is my luggage, Annette," Shultz replied, pointing to a very small piece of carry-on luggage.

Shultz had packed up his life, moved to America, and was able to fit all his belongings into one small piece of carry-on luggage. As I processed this image, I chuckled within myself, remembering the six pieces of luggage my son Chris took to Washington, DC, to complete a four-month college internship! It amused me how strikingly different the lives of these two young men were.

As we made our way to the car, I realized that this story is much bigger than myself, and that it is a story of how God the Father makes a way for His children! I could feel the tangible love of the Father for Shultz, and it made me cry. It was as though I was unexpectedly engulfed by a deep understanding of God's loving-kindness, inundated by the vastness of it. It was God showing me who He is and how His lavish love had the capacity to scoop people out of difficult circumstances—no matter how hard or deep the valley!

Shultz

When I saw Annette and her husband, Gordon, who had come to pick me up at the airport in Boston, I remember smiling so much and for so long that I had a headache. On the way to Annette and Gordon's home, it felt like I was watching a movie, except that I was actually living in one! The sight of skyscrapers; clean, orderly roads; and nicely drawn cities only added to this feeling. That first day in America, Gordon, Annette, and I stayed up late and chatted about my journey and all that had happened. I could not believe that I was to sleep in a real bed in a clean, peaceful house.

I woke up the next morning to chirping birds outside my window. I looked outside and was taken by how geometrically structured and organized the neighborhood was—how the houses had flawless lawns, beautiful plants—and the trees were so well maintained. It was a beautiful sight to behold. I had never seen anything like it, so much so that it brought tears to my eyes! One thing was certain: God was showing me His goodness in a tangible way.

CHAPTER 6

Arriving in America

There are far, far better things ahead
than any we leave behind.

—C. S. Lewis

Annette

Going to Haiti was where I was first exposed to the extreme poverty and suffering of the developing world. The sights and sounds and the quality of everyday Haitian life are etched in my memory; and the images of struggle, desperation, and survival have marked me profoundly. Having been to Haiti had helped me gain some understanding of where Shultz had come from, and also what he had left behind. Coming from middle-class American life, I felt I had so much to learn from the Haitian people and so much to come to understand about Shultz.

When Shultz arrived in America, I realized that it was now time for him to experience my world. What an incredible experience it was to "see" my world through the eyes of another! The things I took for granted and even stopped seeing altogether were now the topic of delightful conversation. Everything in America was new and different for Shultz. It is one thing to see American life in a movie but quite another to actually experience living in the United States. It was the simple things that started conversations, which in turn brought Gordon, Shultz, and myself the most joy and made room for so much laughter.

One day I walked into the kitchen at home and saw Shultz opening and closing the freezer door. Intrigued by what was going on, I stood for a minute or so and watched. Shultz opened the freezer door, looked inside the freezer, closed the door, opened the door again, then looked inside yet again. It appeared as though Shultz wanted to be sure of what he was seeing as he was fascinated by it.

"This is amazing, Annette!" exclaimed Shultz.

"Which part is amazing, Shultz?" I asked.

"The ice—I have never seen anything quite like it!" replied Shultz.

"Really?" I continued

"Ice is so rare in Haiti."

"And here there is so much of it!" I answered.

Simple things such as having ice available in the refrigerator door was something taken for granted in most American households, but for Shultz, it was a shocking sight. Ice is something we never think twice about in America, but to Shultz, it was spectacular phenomenon.

Other things that were new and much appreciated by Shultz were faucets with potable water, a shower with clean running water at the turn of a knob, a toilet inside the house that flushed, a microwave oven that heats things in seconds, having separate bedrooms and a bed with sheets that turn down. To add to this, having screens on the windows that keep the bugs out, as well as having carpeted floors, were new and wonderful to Shultz. Shultz would often walk around the house just to experience the softness of the carpet under his feet. Those early days were filled with fond moments and bursts of laughter!

As Shultz was staying in our home for the first few weeks, I had told him that he was free to eat anything he wanted to eat from the refrigerator. On one particular morning, Shultz was eating a chicken wing and a hamburger roll for breakfast. For a moment, I found myself wanting to correct him and to let him know that the foods he was eating were not breakfast foods. I then realized that I was the one who needed to be corrected. Hunger does not know the difference between what to eat for breakfast, lunch, or dinner. After this occurrence, I realized that I had never stopped to think about hunger before. I had never once stopped to think about food in the way a hungry person thinks about food. Of course, I knew that if you eat, you live; and if you do not eat, eventually you could die—but I had never missed a meal in all my life, unless by choice. *What could I possibly understand about being hungry?*

From my mission trips to Haiti, I came to understand that thousands and thousands of Haitians go to bed every night in a state of extreme hunger and thirst. I also came to understand that first world countries assign a very different value to food. What a luxury to decide that eggs and toast are for breakfast, turkey sandwiches are for lunch, meat and potatoes are for dinner. Hungry people would never decide such a thing. *But what if you were starving?* In that case, you eat any food you can find, whenever you can find it.

The first few weeks after Shultz's arrival were the most gratifying for me. My husband, Gordon, and I realized that all of our hard work had paid off, and we were experiencing the joy of having a son from Haiti in our home. I loved every moment of it, especially when I had the chance of showing Shultz all that his new life in America had to offer. Taking Shultz to see his new living arrangement, which was in a Christian community home, his new university, his new city and church, made the end of that summer and the start of his new life full of hope and anticipation.

As September was drawing near and classes were about to begin, Shultz literally needed a whole new wardrobe to attend the university. Shultz came to America with literally nothing. I decided it would be good to take Shultz to the mall. When he entered the mall for the very first time, the look on Shultz's face was one of utter astonishment! He had simply never seen so many stores and so many clothes of different brands, sizes, designs, and colors in his life. There were so many choices and so many options. It was the sheer sight of North American luxury. Buying him bags full of clothes was so much fun.

As Shultz was settling into life in America, I often wondered if he was happy. I knew he was happy to be in America, but was he happy in his heart? Was America all he had hoped for? Shultz had a lot of opportunity here, but did he feel connected to his new family, and did he miss his family in Haiti? I often asked myself such questions. After all, Shultz was so far away from the place he called home—away from his mom, his sister, and extended family. I felt responsible to make sure he was settling in well, feeling loved and feeling that he was part of our family and our community. We did our best to be sure that he had all he needed to succeed and excel.

CHAPTER 7

◆

The American Dream

Faith is taking the first step even when
you don't see the whole staircase.
—Martin Luther King Jr.

But the path of the just is like the shining sun,
that shines ever brighter unto the perfect day.
—Proverbs 4:18 (NKJV)

Shultz

I remember my very first day at Southern New Hampshire University like it was yesterday. It was late August as I looked around the campus, savoring all that my eye could capture of the vast college grounds. Classes had not yet begun, so I had some time to observe the campus around me. The bushes outside Robert Frost Hall were dancing with the morning breeze. Some students were sitting on the grass, chatting with their friends, while others biked their way through the campus. The atmosphere was friendly and relaxed. As I took a deep breath and inhaled the fresh air, a rush of cool oxygen filled my lungs. I recall thinking to myself, *Wow, this is what a new beginning feels like.* I was both nervous and excited. I still could not believe that I, D'Meza Shultz Pierre Louis, had the chance to attend this university!

As I observed, all the conversations around me were in English. I spoke French and Creole, and I could write, speak, and understand both English and Spanish. But now I had a new challenge: I needed to make myself understood in English to native speakers of English. For this, I needed to complete a language studies course, one which was designed for those who would go on to take courses at the graduate level. While I was still in Haiti, Annette was the first English native speaker I had ever spoken to. In hindsight, my accent was strong, and my sentences were hard to understand.

For the first few weeks of my new graduate language studies course, I would go home after each class in a state of panic. My head would hurt as I had this terrible thought that I was going to fail the course. I was anxious because I knew I was forced to speak only in English just about everywhere. This was stressful as it sometimes made me feel stuck when I felt that I was not able to express myself clearly. For several weeks, the pressure to become better at speaking English pushed me to improve in both speaking and listening skills. I was relieved to see that I was not the only one in my class who was striving to improve on speaking English. Graduate students from all over the world who were enrolled in the same course were going through a similar struggle. Frankly, I was relieved that I wasn't the worst in the class. At the same time, I was overjoyed that every so often, some of my assignments were used by the professor as an example for other students to follow. This encouraged me to believe that I could excel in my new academic environment.

After completing the graduate language school program, I officially started a two-year masters of business administration program (MBA). Upon starting the program, I wanted to finish it in a year. Little did I know how hard that was going to be! The good news was that, unlike college in Haiti, where you lacked the basics to support you, Southern New Hampshire University was fully equipped to help students make the most of their college education. I was amazed at how organized the faculty, as well as my program, was. Books were available on reserve at the college library, where students had access to material from virtually any scholar in the world. The internet connection on campus was always working, along with the electricity without any interruptions or power outages. Professors showed up consistently to class to teach and finish the entire course curriculum. I was in awe of the level of excellence at the university and how the administration cared and paid so much attention to every detail of student life. Students received above and beyond the basic necessities for higher education!

Half of my time studying was spent at Legacy House, the community home in which I lived, and the other half at the lovely home of Bob and Patti, friends from church, where I was treated like a son. As the semester progressed, there were days I would stay in my room like a mad scientist and devour course material since I was taking twice the course load. I was thankful that my roommates from the Legacy House were both understanding and considerate to my need for long hours of study and solitude. I would go for days without seeing my friends or doing extracurricular activities but instead gave much of my time to studying and preparing assignments and term papers. My routine was structured and orderly because life in North America is orderly! Unlike in Haiti, I no longer had to cram in study hours because of the unpredictability of electricity, the bus schedule, road traffic, and school demonstrations. I was also thankful that I had the chance to enjoy the coziness of having my own room for the very first time. I was thankful that I could sit on the carpet in my room and contemplate the small things in life that bring joy, such as opening the window to let in a rush of fresh, clean air!

I was pleasantly surprised that I could work while I took courses at the university. It did not take me long to get accepted as a tutor to undergraduate students in the subjects of math, statistics, economics, accounting, and finance. With a tutoring hourly rate of $9.25 per hour, I had a foretaste of what life would be like in the United States if you work hard. I was shocked to find out that my hourly pay rate as a tutor in America was equivalent to a week's worth of pay in Haiti!

Growing up, I never dreamed about going anywhere else besides the United States. The history of the country, what it stands for, and how it provides the opportunities needed for individuals to reach their full potential is astonishing! These factors enabled me to finish a two-year masters of business administration program in about fifteen months with a grade point average (GPA) of 3.9. During my studies, I made some great friends along the way, learned a lot, and am still learning some valuable lessons. While still a student at Southern New Hampshire University, I felt the care and provision of God through the Haitian Community Center, where I made friends. I also felt cared for through a fund-raising event organized by St. Anselm's College through the Meelia Center for Community Engagement, where I was the main recipient of their legendary wiffle-ball tournament! Donations came from everywhere to help me through my time at the university. I will forever be grateful to everyone who helped me achieve my dream! Overall, completing a master's program was challenging, and completing my degree was extremely fulfilling! I graduated with my MBA in May 2012 and could not wait to enter the workforce and start making money.

Shortly after graduating and starting my first professional job, I met my future wife, Chantel. When I first met her, Chantel had a Jesus tattoo on her left arm, which gave me the opportunity to start up a conversation with her and invite her to my church. Chantel had just moved to Manchester, and she was looking for a home church. I remember looking at Chantel's smile and seeing her love for life glowing through her. The obstacles I had to overcome in my twenty-seven years on earth felt minute in comparison to all the hoops that Chantel had to jump through to stay alive and keep believing in God's promises for her life—she is a true warrior!

The more I came to know Chantel, the more I realized she was God's provision for my life! Her passion for life was infectious, and there was never a dull moment with her.

According to my mom, it was the perfect time to pursue getting married. Unlike in the United States where your age dictates your maturity, in Haiti, regardless of your age or maturity, everything is based on your ability to support yourself. Since I had just graduated and I had my first serious job at the bank, meeting Chantel was perfect! Before I knew it, Chantel and I were in prewedding counseling with Annette and Gordon Tuttle! The rest is history. Chantel and I got married, bought a home, and had three beautiful children.

~ ~ ~

Never Forget Where You Come From

Shortly after starting our new family, Chantel desired to keep God at the center of our lives. Reading the Bible together and learning Bible verses by heart was part of our routine. We memorized passages like the Lord's Prayer, the Bible's golden rule, and Psalm 23 by heart. We also tried to incorporate prayer in our daily schedule as much as we could. When Chantel and I met with the immigration officer to finalize our papers, my wife and I were interviewed separately. Interestingly enough, the officer at the USCIS office, testing our claims that we were Christians, asked me to recite Psalms 23. *That is a piece of cake*, I thought to myself. After the interview, my wife told me she was asked to recite Psalm 23 as well. As Chantel spoke, a strange feeling shook me to the core. It was as if God was making His presence felt, proving once more that He was in my US citizenship process.

By July 2012, I started working as a teller for TD Bank. There I learned a lot about the banking system, the importance of customer service, and how much harder I will have to work to prove myself. As an immigrant, my accent did not help me in this process. My genuine interest in caring for people was consequential in helping me move forward in my career. Obstacles were overcome, and one and a half years later, I moved onto a bigger opportunity at JP Morgan Chase. Two years later, after rumors of how my department would move out of state, I changed jobs again to work at Fidelity Investments. Armed with my MBA, I earned my series 7, 63 and 66.[1]

---

[1] These are licenses issued by FINRA (Financial Industry Regulatory Authority) in the United States allowing the holder to sell some securities products and to act as an investment advisor representative.

Now I am studying to be a certified financial planner which is abbreviated as CFP. I currently work as a workplace planning consultant, where I interact daily with clients who wish to build a plan for retirement and nonretirement goals. I help design investment strategies to reach those goals based on their financial situation, timeline, and risk tolerance so they can focus on what matters most to them. Enabling others to create wealth for themselves and prosper is personally a rewarding experience for me. I am still pondering upon how my knowledge fits into the big picture of God's plan for my life. However, I am fully persuaded that God brought me to the United States for a reason, and I am convinced that my hands-on knowledge will be used for a greater purpose that is unfolding gradually, one that will benefit society on a greater level.

I've come to believe that the human mind cannot fully grasp or fathom all that God has planned for us. While I was living in Haiti, I believed I was living the life God had for me. I took concrete steps to slowly but surely do what I felt in my heart was God's plan for my life. Then an earth-shattering natural disaster destroyed everything I had worked for. The good news is that God never leaves us nor forsakes us, and through Him, we can rebuild and move into even greater things.

The fullness of what lies ahead for me, my family, and Haiti is ever unfolding. However, I am convinced that as I yield my life to Jesus and to His plans and purposes, He will not only lead me in the right direction but rescue me out of every trial and tribulation. I am not only a recipient of an exceptional rescue mission; I am a recipient of His extravagant love, mercy, and grace. I know that when God asks me to cross a sea blindfolded on the promise that my feet will not get wet, it because He has already split the waters. I stand in faith and press on so I can enter the land He has promised me. Jesus is so present, so real, so tangible to ever quit believing in God's master plan for my life. Life has, and will continue to throw surprises my way. What is reassuring is that I know how the story will end because the victory was already won at the cross of Calvary over two thousand years ago.

What lies beyond the furthest horizon that my eye can see? As I take one step at a time, the path is becoming clearer, and the shadow of unknowns is being dispelled by pure Light.

◆

CHAPTER 8

Be the Answer to Your Own Prayers

For God has not given us a spirit of fear, but of
power and of love and of a sound mind.
—1 Timothy 1:7 (NKJV)

Annette

Growing up in a large Irish Italian Catholic family, I always knew there was a God. I knew *about* Jesus because I saw Him dead on the cross every Sunday at church. I knew He was God, but I was pretty sure that He didn't know me. I remember that I wanted to please Him and that when I would sin, I would feel full of remorse and was afraid of punishment. I remember wanting to be "right" with Him, but I had no idea how to reach Jesus, and I had no idea if He would accept me even if I did.

As the years went on, I searched for purpose and direction in my life. I didn't want to live in sin, and I didn't want to live a selfish or self-centered life. I felt a constant pull on my heart to live outside of myself. I had a deep desire to live a life other than the one I was living. My life was good—some would even say blessed—but I knew there was something else, something more. I can look back now and see that God was calling and wooing me into the life He had planned for me since the beginning of time. The God-size hole in my heart was about to be filled with God's plan for me.

Psalm 139:16, says, "Your eyes saw my substance being yet unformed, and in Your book they all were written, the days fashioned for me when as yet there were none of them." Imagine such a thing—that God has planned your days before you were even born!

I remember the day back in 1986 when I, a lost and broken girl, a sinner, was rescued by a loving God. The Gospel of Jesus is a powerful thing, and it changed my life forever. Jesus was no longer dead on the cross; He was alive and real and calling me to live my life through Him. What I had been searching for all along was found in Jesus. To be awakened by His love and ushered into a life of love, peace, joy, purpose, and most importantly, servanthood was to find out who I really was and why I was born. I stopped searching for significance in the things of the world and instead fully stepped into God's plan for my life. Oh, what a joy to live a life outside of myself and to be fully alive.

It became my prayer that my book in heaven would be opened and that I would be on the right page at the right time. My continuing prayer is that I will live my life as God has planned.

The Bible also says in Jeremiah 29:11, "For I know the thoughts that I think towards you, says the Lord, thoughts of peace and not of evil, to give you a future and a hope." Very early on in my walk with Jesus, this scripture ignited something wonderful in my heart and mind. To think that

God had a plan for me and I no longer had to make a way for myself, but instead just say yes to His plan—my new life in Christ offered me a freedom I had never known.

As the days and years passed, the revelation of what Jesus had done for me and what He had rescued me from became a constant source of motivation in my heart, and I wanted that for everyone. Clearly, what He had done for me, He would do for everyone. I wanted to give Jesus everything: my time, my money, my talents, my abilities, my very life. As I began a daily surrendering of my old life to fully apprehend my new life, I could never have imagined all that He had planned for me.

> The Spirit of the Lord God is upon Me, because the Lord has anointed Me to preach good tidings to the poor; He has sent Me to heal the brokenhearted, to proclaim liberty to the captives, and the opening of the prison to those who are bound; to proclaim the acceptable year of the Lord, and the day of vengeance of our God; to comfort all who mourn in Zion, to give them beauty for ashes, the oil of joy for mourning, the garments of praise for the spirit of heaviness; that they may be called trees of righteousness, the planting of the Lord, that He may be glorified. (Isaiah 61:1–3)

> For everyone to whom much is given, from him much will be required; and to whom much has been committed, of him they will ask the more. (Luke 12:48)

I am that person, and you probably are too. The one that "much was given" and to "whom much has been committed." That means that much is required of us, and much will be asked.

As time passed, God was constantly pulling on my heart to serve Him in ways that I never imagined, especially on short-term missions. This meant, however, that I needed to overcome lots of fears and apprehension that resided in my heart. I was afraid of everything! When we purpose to serve the Lord and live out all that He is calling us to do, we can bet that the enemy of our souls will try to stop us.

Every summer, my husband and two sons would vacation at a resort in New Hampshire. One beautiful summer day, we decided to take the ski slope chairlift to the top of a small mountain and spend the afternoon hiking down. The views from the chairlift were gorgeous, and we were excited to begin our little adventure.

About midway up the mountain with my husband sitting next to me, I heard a menacing voice that said, *You are afraid of heights*. I immediately took a deep breath and leaned back against my husband's arm that rested on the back of the chair. Fear permeated my whole being. I was thrown into an all-out panic attack and could hardly breathe. I realized that this voice was the voice of the enemy, and my mind tried to process what was happening. The response inside my head was, *I am?* as I kept this arrow of accusation from entering my heart. I remember saying to myself, *I'm forty-three years old, and I've never been afraid of heights*. How is it now that the enemy wants me to think I was afraid of heights?

The next ten minutes were a nightmare. My son Chris was sitting on the seat ahead of us by himself. As I looked at him, I realized that he had not lowered the safety bar, and he was leaning forward in the seat, enjoying the beautiful view.

Panic filled my heart as the enemy told me he would fall out. At the same time, I looked down at the mountain below us, only to see huge granite boulders that had been exposed by dynamite. Immediately, in my fear and panic, all I could imagine was that Chris was going to fall out of the chair and be impaled by the granite spikes below. My spirit was calling out to Jesus as I tried to breathe.

As if that wasn't bad enough, the chairlift came to a complete stop, and we were now suspended in midair. Off to our right, we could see and hear a thunderstorm rolling in over the mountains. I was completely undone. I was stranded in the air on a metal chairlift, having a panic attack, and now a thunderstorm was approaching. After what seemed like an eternity, the chairlift began to move, and we arrived at the top of the mountain. We made our way down the mountain path in a relentless rainstorm, ducking in and out of the forest to avoid the rain.

That experience on the mountain and the accusation from the enemy that I was afraid of heights propelled me into a yearlong battle of overcoming fear. The enemy was not giving up his relentless fight to keep me from God's plan for my life. I could never have imagined all the ways that the "suggestion" that I was "afraid of heights" would affect my life. I spent a whole year overcoming that demonic voice. Every time I drove across a bridge, entered an elevator, stood on a balcony, or thought to fly in an airplane, I had to battle the spirit of fear.

That year, I knew that I wasn't just fighting against fear; I was fighting for God's plan for my life: a life of missions. I knew that if I didn't overcome this fear, I would live a small paralyzed life, and I refused to do that.

One day as I was reading the Bible, Holy Spirit highlighted a pathway to freedom from fear. First Samuel 17 tells an amazing story of a young David standing before a huge

Philistine giant named Goliath. For forty days, morning and evening, Goliath would taunt the army of Israel, "If he is able to fight with me and kill me, then we will be your servants. But if I prevail against him and kill him, then you shall be our servants and serve us."

Why was a young David the one who stepped up to fight Goliath? Why not his brothers or other leaders in the armies of Israel? David stepped into the battle with Goliath because he knew that God had a plan for his life. First Samuel 16 recounts the story of David being anointed king over Israel. David knew God's plan for his life, and he was not about to become a servant to the Philistines. Holy Spirit spoke similar words to me: *Annette, your mission field is on the other side of your fear.* The lost, the broken, the homeless, the impoverished were waiting for me. The enemy knew that if I was afraid of heights, then I would not fly. I knew right then that if I was to fly around the world on mission, then I would have to overcome fear. That year, I learned so much about the power of the Word of God as our weapon to overcome the attacks of the enemy and to stand until our victory comes. Shortly after my victory, I was invited on a mission trip to Ukraine on what would become the first of many trips to Eastern Europe, and to many other nations around the world.

God has released a bravery in my heart to answer the call to go anywhere He asks me to go. I want to encourage you not to let fear hinder God's plan for your life. On the other side of your fear and anxiety is the abundant life God has written in your book.

If I had not overcome fear, I would never have met Shultz!

Watch, stand fast in the faith, be brave, be strong.
—1 Corinthians 16:13 (NKJV)

CHAPTER 9

◆

Vision International Missions and the Mission on La Gonave Island

Go into all the world and preach the
gospel to every creature.
—Mark 16:15 (NKJV)

If Jesus Christ is God and died for me, then no
sacrifice can be too great for me to make for Him.
—C. T. Studd

Are you looking to go on an adventure and leave your mark in history? Are you looking for new opportunities to make the love of God known in a real way that makes a difference in the lives of others? Then this is your opportunity to go on a mission trip to work with the Ti Palmiste Community Children's Home on La Gonâve Island, Haiti, via Vision International Missions!

After the earthquake in 2010, the death toll in Haiti was estimated to be 230,000 people. It was estimated that before the earthquake, there were nearly 400,000 orphans. After the earthquake, that number swelled to nearly 1,000,000 children without parents. The need for orphanages was looming large in the aftermath of the quake, and it was decided that Vision International Missions would establish an orphanage on the island of La Gonâve.

La Gonâve is the island in which Shultz was born and raised. It is located off the coast of Haiti with a population of approximately ninety thousand people. After a two-hour ferry ride, it is at the port of Anse-à-Galets that the real adventure begins and where Haitian life can be seen and experienced. La Gonâve is a wonderful adventure! It lacks in basic modern conveniences like electricity, water, plumbing, or sanitation of any kind. Roads are a challenge and often dangerous. It is a land of striking contrasts. Its landscape is a combination of little villages that seem rather normal but also shacks tucked away in the thicket. Surrounded by the bluest sky you will ever see, the island's beaches and mountains are breathtaking. It is here where nature's beauty is intertwined with profound poverty. The island has unique Caribbean island qualities, and yet trash and garbage line its shores. New concrete houses are being constructed next to the rubble of a home once occupied.

Reverend Kenneth Whitten, director of Vision International Missions, had been ministering in Haiti on the main island since 1983, but his work was about to take a big turn. VIM is an interdenominational, nonprofit Christian organization that serves where others often will not go. Mission trips with VIM are an adventure in of themselves and are sometimes what one might call mission camping: sleeping in churches, long rides to poor villages, and living lean for a week. When you serve in remote areas, you make the best of what you can bring in and what is available (not all trips are like this, but it is certainly the case in Haiti). VIM brings the love of God along on each mission and partners with in-country missions to identify where the need is greatest. Mission trips generally support physical, medical, and spiritual needs of Haitians.

Ken had often partnered with a local pastor in Haiti, Pastor Samuel Merisier, to identify where in Haiti VIM would run medical clinics and spread the Word and love of God. On one of these mission trips, Pastor Samuel asked if VIM would consider crossing the bay to the island of La Gonâve to go up the mountain to a small village called Ti Palmiste. Pastor Samuel has his home in La Gonâve and has planted a church there. It is in this village that Pastor Samuel Merisier noticed that there were children who were scavengers, just scraping by, lacking parenting, shelter, and access to food. He had a heart's desire to open an orphanage but had no support to do so. VIM's first trip to Ti Palmiste was planned, and shortly thereafter, on the grounds of the Bethel Church that Pastor Samuel had planted, the Ti Palmiste Community Orphanage (TCO) was opened. While dorm rooms were being constructed, children began to show up, asking when the orphanage would be ready.

TCO was opened in 2011 to thirty-four children aged two to eleven years old. Some children were orphaned, some had single parents, some had parents but were neglected due to poverty, while others due to illness of all kinds. Melissa, Ken Whitten's niece, who went to Haiti in 2010 with us and the rest of Ken Whitten team, had her life completely changed from one mission trip! Not only did God bring Shultz to America, but He called Melissa to Haiti as a full-time missionary to run the children's home on the island of Ti Palmiste. No one could have seen that coming! Only God could make all these things happen! Over the years, Melissa Saint Cyr (now married to Shultz's cousin Lender) and Vision

International Missions (VIM) have focused on meeting the basic needs of the children, where food, shelter, education, health, clothing, and the spiritual needs of the children are provided for.

Over time, VIM has focused fund-raising efforts to provide financial support through monthly sponsorships for the operating and capital expenses of running such a facility. Quarterly mission trips from the United States were started with each team addressing some particular need at TCO and for the community of Ti Palmiste whenever possible. Since 2011, VIM has seen thirteen children on La Gonâve Island reunite with a family member, and there are twenty-one children now remaining at the orphanage. TCO also had its name changed to *Ti Palmiste Children's Home* to more closely reflect that some of the children are not orphaned.

Many mission team members from the United States have made repeated visits to Ti Palmiste as their hearts were filled with the prospect of giving hope for a bright future to this small group of children. Mission team members felt as though they left a little of themselves behind with each mission trip, and eagerly sought the bright smiles and slightly larger children when they returned the following year. It is wonderful to see children flourish as love pours into them. Watching the children's health improve, their bodies grow, and their hearts learn about the love of God, is a sustaining factor in such a hard place to operate.

Since 2011 and the initial building of the dorm rooms, the dorms have been expanded to cater to the need of having larger living spaces for the growing children. A dining room, mission office, two wells with pumps, vocational studies room (for sewing, computer education, and remedial studies) were built, and new roofing was installed on all the buildings. Teams have also installed gutters to funnel rainwater into a cistern, painted rooms, built shelving, built beds, cleared land for small gardens, built jungle gyms, and brought countless pieces of underwear, clothing, backpacks, and hygiene supplies. It is a world of effort for sure!

As sponsorships change, funding for the Ti Palmiste Children's Home is always a bit of a challenge, as there are always unexpected needs that arise. There have been multiple hospital visits for fevers, infections, and the usual happenings with active children. Education is not provided by the government, so each year, additional funding is needed for tuition, uniforms, and supplies.

If you would like to get involved with the *Ti Palmiste Children's Home*, whether through a mission trip or with financial support for operating or capital expenses, please reach out to

Reverend Ken Whitten
Tel: +1 603-867-9955
Email: vimissions@aol.com.
Or visit our website: www.vimissions.com

To book Annette Tuttle for speaking engagements
or to order more copies of *Against All Odds*,

e-mail annettetuttle2222@gmail.com.

ABOUT THE AUTHOR

◆

Annette Tuttle has served the Lord for over thirty years. During those years, she has been active in intercession and prayer ministry for her church, city, state, and the nation. She founded two houses of prayer: Symphony House of Prayer and Capital City House of Prayer. In addition, she is a Christian speaker and teacher. Her passion, however, is short-term missions work. She has been on over twenty-five short-term missions trips around the world. As of the writing of this book, she has returned to Haiti seven times.

CPSIA information can be obtained
at www.ICGtesting.com
Printed in the USA
LVHW041217110820
662878LV00003B/408